Sorcerer

Ed Atkins & Steven Zultanski

D1571063

I once compared *Sorcerer* to a Harold Pinter play. But Pinter never instructed you on how to dismantle your face, amplify your house plumbing, levitate your computer, dance with your sofa, or place a penknife on a bed so that it appears as if no one put it there. Atkins and Zultanski's play redesigns the contemporary home as a machine for comedy, sadness, and anxiety. *Sorcerer* is a unique work of theatre and literature, beautiful and unsettling. I can only relate it to the words of the late, great Angela Lansbury: 'My family always said I'd travel anywhere to put on a false nose.'

   – DAN FOX

Sorcerer is the emphatic magic of lived-time actions. Those innocuous motions, felt and repeated, held in the muscular memory of our bodies and eyes and viscerally present. That we cannot see, but here, for a slowed minute, might feel in the familiarity of an action so often performed as to be invisible as an action at all. This is a dialogue between the object body and other objects, so distended and loud as to be near silent. Where each action held might also begin to corrupt, or stain, pulling too hard, tuning in and tearing out. A politics of who we are in how we are, learnt, programmed, actioned, and acted, felt and not always forlorn.

   – GHISLAINE LEUNG

In this ingenious work, Zultanski and Atkins innovatively deploy both material and human gesture to paint a sad yet almost comic scenario of contemporaneity. While a group of friends conduct inane conversation about subjects like how to take off your pants, the material objects in the apartment bump and grind as if Satie's *Musique d'ameublement* has come to life. The interminable redundancy of radios, kettles, radiators, squeaking, hissing, etc., finally dominate the set in a way that is as flat and nondescript as the friends' conversation. Yet these people raise serious compassion in us, for they are us. Atkins and Zultanski's brand of drolly underwrought utterance shows us once more that innovative device is the *sine qua non* of really good art.

– GAIL SCOTT

Vivid on the page, *Sorcerer* is a surprising and compelling hallucinatory theatre text for a cast of three. In it a set of hyper-naturalistic micro-conversations are laid out in an unblinking deadpan; crisp dialogues that focus in on the body, mapping the detail of daily actions and experiences from the removal of clothing, to the acquisition of new skills, and the precise interior feeling of headaches. Meanwhile, in a dynamic counterpoint to all the talk, a series of playful and increasingly strange physical transformations of the performers and the space they inhabit are proposed. Atkins and Zultanski have made the score for a complex, haunting event.

– TIM ETCHELLS

With *Sorcerer*, Ed Atkins and Steven Zultanski invite us 'round for an evening of conversational bricolage, word games, and mild social debarment (with grapes). As guests, we are welcomed to an inanimate space, every bit as active as the gathering held within it, and duly reminded of the potential infallibility of a mixed company setting. We are privy to the trivial crosscut with the vital; we submit to compression fetish and sulphuric mythology; we ruminate on the merits of facial deconstruction, and most crucially of all, we are reminded once again about the awful sad joy of humanness and what it means to be alone.

– GRAHAM LAMBKIN

Sorcerer 15

Sorcerer was originally a play commissioned by Rikke Hedeager and staged at Copenhagen's Teater Revolver from 19 March to 9 April, 2022. It starred Lotte Andersen, Peter Christoffersen, and Ida Cæcilie Rasmussen, with choreography by Nønne Mai Svalholm. The dialogue was constructed from conversations between dear friends, recorded over a few months. A film adaptation of the stage production, also directed by us, exists. This book version is its own thing—a literary object independent of the play as well as a guide to staging it.

Sorcerer

Three friends—IDA, LOTTE, and PETER—are in a studio apartment.

In the apartment, there's a kitchen, a dining table and chairs, and a living room area with a couch and an armchair and a TV and a coffee table. There are also other things, such as two lamps, one on each side of the room, a hatstand with coats on it, and a front door.

On the dining table, there's a thermos, an open laptop, a set of keys, and a printer cartridge. (SEE APPENDIX C.)

At the back of the room in the centre of the room, there's a vast screen/mirror thing, a few metres square. It acts just like the magnifying side of a shaving mirror. When something passes in front of it or comes close to it, its image is projected large. (SEE APPENDIX D.)

Also, in the corner of the apartment, there's a double bed with squirming sheets. The sheets continuously writhe without discernible pattern. (SEE APPENDIX I.)

The room has three radiators. They are connected by pipes and they are warm because the radiators are on. (SEE APPENDIX A.)

The three friends are talking. IDA is sitting on the couch and LOTTE is in the armchair. PETER is in the kitchen area getting some beers. They seem to know each other well, like friends.

PETER'S a bit under the weather. Not too much. He coughs occasionally as they talk.

> LOTTE
> *(motions putting on a t-shirt, really fast, not accurate, almost like putting on a hat that goes down to her neck.)*
> Like this?
> *(still doing motion.)*
> Like this?

> IDA
> Yeah, I always put my head through first, so the shirt hangs from my neck, kind of like a big floppy necklace, and then I find the arms.

> PETER
> *(from the kitchen.)*
> Hm.

> LOTTE
> I do the opposite. I put my arms through and then my head.

> IDA
> How do you do that?

> LOTTE
> I put my arms through like this—
> *(makes motion, puts her hands through the air like a long glove or like putting hands in a cow, one after the other.)*
> and then I do—

(swooping motion, ducks head in, almost like going under a short doorway.)

PETER
(as he's carrying the beers over.)
I do an awkward mixture of both. I put my head and one arm through at the same time—
(makes motion, half-lifts one arm and tilts head, like putting head through and checking on the other side of a portal.)
so that the shirt is halfway on and it's a little tight, it's—

IDA
Like a diagonal—

PETER
Yeah, it's criss-crossing my body, and it's constricting—
(constricts body, not accurate to putting on a shirt.)
so I have to push my other arm through to pull the rest of it on—
(back to putting on a shirt—one arm is up, body twisting like it's trying to get into a hole it doesn't fit into.)
and then it doesn't sit quite right on my body because it's all twisted around me—
(constricts again, but with arm up.)

LOTTE
Yeah—

IDA
Yeah.

PETER
(*walking back to kitchen area with grapes in a bowl for
everyone to snack on.*)
So then I have to untwist it—
(*pulls at shirt, untwisting.*)
you know, pull it into shape and shake it a little—
(*shakes shirt.*)
to get it into shape.

PETER puts the bowl of grapes on the coffee table and
sits down again with the others. He relaxes into the
couch and it crinkles because it's made of old leather.
As he settles in, it crinkles more. Both of his feet are
flat on the floor and he's wearing socks. The other two
friends are wearing shoes. PETER'S socks are thin and
purple. They are the last socks in the world.

IDA
There's a way people do it in the movies, which I
copied as a kid: you put your arms in first—
(*puts arms in.*)
and you go—
(*pulls over head in a movie way.*)

LOTTE
Yeah, that's basically how I do it. But less gracefully
than in the movies.

IDA
Is that how you take it off, too?

                          LOTTE
Yeah.

                           IDA
That's definitely how someone in a movie would
take it off—

                          PETER
Because it shows off the torso—

                           IDA
Exactly.

                          LOTTE
Hm.

                           IDA
I've never done it like that. I ruin all the collars of
my shirts, because I grab the collar, and I do this—
      (*pulls at collar, like a tortoise retreating into its shell,
      yanking at the elastic.*)
and then work my way up like this—
      (*pulls up over her head, stretching the collar, so it's like
      she's looking out of a little cave.*)
it's awful.

                          PETER
Yeah, yeahyeah, I get that. I don't ruin the collars but
I often rip the armholes. Because I put one hand—
      (*pulls down at armpit, like opening armpit.*)

LOTTE

Yeah—

PETER

I put one hand up into the shirt, and pull the armpit down—
   (*continues to pull at armpit.*)
so that the armpit hole is wider—
   (*stretches it.*)
and then I pull my elbow through—
   (*pulls down elbow through armpit hole.*)

LOTTE

That's so inefficient. I do it very cleanly, like this—
   (*crosses arms at bottom of shirt and then uncrosses them
   into the air like wings, clicks fingers like 'ta-da.'*)
but that means that all my shirts are inside out when I drop them on the floor.

IDA

So you pull it off in one fluid motion?

LOTTE

Well, not quite the magic trick of crossed arms—
   (*makes motion again but more gracefully.*)
but more like peeling it off. And then it ends up inverted.

IDA

Yes, yes. I can see that. I leave shirts on the floor too, but only some of them are inside out.

And some of them are half inside out. I don't
even know how that happens.

LOTTE

Huh.

Pretty often, all three friends take a sip of their beers or
they reach across the table to grab a grape from the bowl
of grapes. At one point, IDA fumbles a grape and drops
it onto the table, then quickly picks it up off the table
and puts it in her mouth.

IDA

And the same with my trousers. One leg will be
inside out, but not the other one.

PETER

But that makes sense to me because trousers, when
you're taking them off, often one leg will get stuck on
the heel—
    (*motions like he's peeling something off that is stuck on
    his heel.*)
and then that whole leg is yanked inside out.

LOTTE

I avoid that by pulling them all the way down—
    (*kind of motions her trousers down.*)
and then grabbing the bottom cuff to get my foot
out—
    (*grips cuff.*)
so they don't go inside out.

PETER

I do everything lopsided, apparently. I take one leg
off first—
    (*motions one leg down.*)
you know, I pull one down as far as it can go, and
then I pull the other leg down—
    (*motions pulling other leg down.*)
so the trousers tighten around my legs and they're
hard to pull off. That last tug takes some work.
    (*constricts again, but at the bottom of his body, presses*
    his knees together like someone impersonating a snake,
    then sits back up.)

IDA

How many things do you group together? If you've
got a button-up shirt on and a t-shirt underneath,
like I do now—
    (*little tug.*)
do you pull off both at once? I would take off the
shirt and the t-shirt at the same time.

LOTTE

What, how?

IDA

I would undo a couple of buttons—
    (*undoing buttons motion.*)
and then just pull the whole assembly off.
    (*makes inaccurate motion, like opening ribcage.*)

PETER

Wait. You take your shirt off with your t-shirt?

                              IDA
Yeah.

                            PETER
No.

                              IDA
Yeah. And the same with my trousers. I just take off
my underwear with them. And I pick up my socks on
the way—
        (*slides hands down trousers with a flourish at the end
        like releasing a dove.*)

                            LOTTE
Well, yeah, I do that too. Everyone does that, right?

                            PETER
I think everyone does that.

                              IDA
Maybe—
        (*like she's about to say something more.*)

                            PETER
Though a friend made me these trousers—
        (*delicate pinch at the fabric, being gentle.*)
so I'm careful with them.

                            LOTTE
They're great.

IDA

Oooh.

PETER

Yeah. I wish I could make something like this.

IDA

Do you ever think about making your own clothes?

PETER

I tried, but the learning curve is so steep.

IDA

Yeah.

PETER

I actually tried to make a shirt once but it's so difficult.

LOTTE

But we say that now, right? But my mother was
always like, 'Oh we're going out this weekend, we'll
just make ourselves some dresses.'

PETER

Yeah.

IDA

Yeah.

LOTTE

I mean, people did that.

IDA

But it takes a lot of practice, that's the thing.

LOTTE

Yeah, yeah.

IDA

My mom told me about her mom, and she would
go to very fancy dinners and things wearing
an immaculate dress that she'd made and designed
and everything.

PETER

Yeah.

IDA

She cut it and sewed it, and it looked / well, I didn't
see it. But each one was unique, you know.

PETER

Of course.

IDA

But she probably learned to sew when she was a kid.
It would be different to start now.

LOTTE

Yeah.

PETER

Yeah.

LOTTE

There's just so many different things to learn how
to do.

IDA

It's true.

PETER

Yeah.

(*a short pause.*)

LOTTE

If you could learn any skill, like wake up tomorrow
and be really good at any one thing, what would it be?

PETER

Great question.

IDA

You don't mean / just to get the criteria straight, you
don't mean like knowing all languages or something?

LOTTE

Yeah, not like, I'd wake up and get three more wishes.
(*inside laugh.*)

IDA

Okay, so it's not like invisibility, or flying, but a skill
that people actually have, right?

PETER

Like a craft.

LOTTE

Yeah.

IDA

I think I'd like to be an incredible carpenter.

LOTTE

Yeah, that's a good one.

IDA

Like incredible. I'll make you anything and it'll be fucking insane.

LOTTE

That'd be cool.

PETER

I wish I could even hang something on my wall without knocking a giant hole in it and destroying the wall.

LOTTE

Does that happen?

PETER

Every time I try to hang something, yeah.

LOTTE

You knock a giant hole in the wall?

PETER

Yeah.

IDA

I've always been good at teaching myself how to do little things like that, like hanging things on walls.

LOTTE

Yeah, but you like to learn things.

IDA

That's true.

LOTTE

I hate to learn anything.

PETER

I like to learn things but I don't. People explain things to me and I just don't understand or I immediately forget. I would like to knit perfectly. I tried to learn but it takes so long.

LOTTE

That would be a good one.

PETER

And I would also like to know how to garden really well.

LOTTE

Gardening, like g—

IDA
(interrupting.)
I'd also quite like to be able—and this is boring—but
I'd like to be able to program really well.

LOTTE
Why? What would you do with that?

IDA
Well, it's basically like inventing tools, right?

PETER
Yeah.

LOTTE
I mean, none of these things are impossible. Like
knitting. You could just do it every night for the next
six months, and you'd be good at it.

PETER
Yeah.

IDA
What about playing music? If I could wake up
tomorrow and really do anything, I think I would
like to play the piano well, or something like that.

LOTTE
Oh, yeah.

IDA

I would like virtuosic songwriting ability. To be able
to translate thoughts and feelings into a song.

PETER

What kind of song?

IDA sings her song. It is a long, gradually ascending tone
like a siren that only goes up. It doesn't particularly
sound like it's coming from her. She doesn't really move
her eyes or mouth. She just sits there until it's over. Her
voice cracks a little at the highest and loudest point,
then she stops abruptly because the song is over, and
takes a breath.

LOTTE

What was that supposed to be?

PETER

What kind of song is that?

IDA

I was just seeing if I have the skill, but I don't.
   (*very slight pause.*)

PETER

   (*little coughing sigh.*)
So when are we going to learn these things?

IDA

I don't know.

LOTTE

I mean, what would it take?

PETER

(*scrunches up his face, mumbles something.*)

IDA

What did you say?

PETER

I can feel my throat closing up.

LOTTE

Are you okay?

PETER

Yeah, yeah, I'm fine.
  (*coughs into his elbow, a bit dramatically.*)
I don't think it would take much. But then why don't
I do something like that now? Learn something new.
I could just learn how to do something.

IDA

Yeah, you really could.

PETER

Though it might be naïve to think that I could just
fancy something and learn how to do it.

IDA

No, it would just be an investment of time, and maybe
years of something, but what—

PETER

And then I think, oh here I go again with a new idea
for a new life. How many times can I do that?

LOTTE

As many times as you want. Why not? What's the
virtue in picking one thing when you were young
and sticking to it?

PETER

No, of course, that's what I'm saying. But I always
wanted to be someone who by this age had done
a lot of different things—

LOTTE

But you are like that—

PETER

Yeah, but I don't feel like I've done any of those things
fully. Though I don't know what that would mean.

LOTTE

Yeah, I don't know what that would mean.

(*a short pause.*)

IDA

I also think that, the more you learn other skills, the
more the skills you have are improved.

LOTTE

Yes.

PETER

That's wise.

(another short pause, they take a sip or two of their drinks.)

PETER

I was thinking today about that story you told me about your dad cracking eggs into a pan and them being black.

IDA

Black eggs?

LOTTE

Mm-hm.

IDA

How do eggs turn black?

LOTTE

I don't know. Really rancid?

IDA

They must be very old eggs. I've never heard of that.

PETER

How is everyone familiar with the smell of rotten eggs? I don't remember ever actually smelling rotten eggs.

IDA

But people describe other smells with it.

PETER

Yeah.

LOTTE

I know what sulphur smells like, and that's supposed
to smell like rotten eggs.

PETER

Yeah, but when have you cracked an egg and it was
rotten? Have you ever actually smelled that?

LOTTE

Never.

PETER

Did you smell your dad's black egg?

LOTTE

No / But I remember it really shocking him, a lot. I
think he was prone to reading signs into things. And
there's nothing more ominous than a black, stinky egg.

PETER AND IDA

   (*looking.*)

LOTTE

I guess he was merrily making himself some lunch,
and the day was destroyed.

IDA

Well, if he read signs into things, that would ruin
the day.

LOTTE

He just saw himself as, 'Of course, I get the black egg.' He was like that.

IDA

Yeah, sure.

LOTTE

He was the kind of person—and it was both true and of course ludicrous—where there'd be a plate of very ripe peaches or something, and he'd pick the only hard one.

IDA

Was that your sense of him, too? Or was that just his sense of himself?

LOTTE

Oh no, it was very clearly his sense of himself. I didn't see him like that. But also, it was a self-fulfilling thing.

IDA

Sure.

PETER

But I get it. I'm...
  (*pause, his face scrunches up like packaging.*)
Ugh, I have a bit of a headache.

  (*slight pause.*)

IDA

Hey / Let's pretend...that I don't know what a
headache is.

LOTTE

Um, it's when you have a pain in your head.

IDA

But no, no, describe it to me.

LOTTE

Oh, okay...
   (*thinking.*)
I almost want to use the word pressure. It's like a bad
feeling personified in pressure. You know that kind of
anxious, pit-of-the-stomach, like, 'I'm-nervous' feeling?

IDA

Yeah.

LOTTE

That nervousness, but in the head.
   (*points at head.*)

PETER

Yeah.

LOTTE

Sometimes, when I get a headache, it feels like
something large is in my skull pounding against
my forehead trying to get out.
   (*makes a knocking-on-a-door motion.*)

PETER

Yeah, a pounding headache.

LOTTE

Or it pulsates.

PETER

Yeah...

LOTTE

Or it feels like your head is being constricted. Like
there's something tied tightly around it, like a rope.
(*makes a tying-a-rope motion, like mooring a boat.*)

PETER

Yeah.

LOTTE

So the pain *is* the built-up pressure.

PETER

Exactly. The pressure.

IDA

Like it's going to burst?

LOTTE

Well, if it did, that would be a relief. But also you
know that it won't burst. It's just going to continue
to build up pressure until it eventually ebbs.

PETER

Oh, yeah.

LOTTE

Also, sometimes the pain radiates around your head.
It doesn't stay in one place.
(*makes motion around head, like drawing a halo.*)
It can even climb down into your neck and shoulders.

IDA

But it's still a headache?

LOTTE

Yeah, because the head is the focus.

PETER

The head is always the focus.

IDA

So it feels like the head is the centre of the body?

LOTTE

Well, I usually feel like that.
(*playing with her hair, drapes some across her face, over
her upper lip, like a moustache.*)
Because, well / when I think of the head, I think of
it as a narrow attic with a triangular shape, it's really
grey and it's made of wooden boards.
(*lets go of hair, it flops down back into its place.*)
And every time I think of a headache, I get this image
of that attic. And I feel like I'm inside of that. I'm
getting compressed in there, I'm being pressed on

all sides, and I can feel it everywhere in my body. And maybe that's because every thought is in my head, and it feels like everything I am is my head, which is all of my body too. So my shoulders and my stomach start hurting, my knees. Even my ankles. Or sometimes it itches between my toes. It's really a full-body experience, because I'm trapped in the attic.

PETER
(*after thinking for a second.*)
I'm also inside of that attic. But it's just the sides of my head that get compressed—
(*holds right hand to right side of his head, maybe an inch from his head, like there was a forcefield there.*)

IDA
Not the top?

PETER
No.

IDA
More like a clamp?

PETER
Yeah, like a clamp.

LOTTE
Do you ever have, like / early morning or late night fantasies of that kind of thing, like a clamp on the side of your head?

PETER

I'm always thinking about a clamp on my head.
I guess I have a lot of compression fantasies.

IDA

Like crushing your head?

PETER

Yeah, something very brutal, like a G-clamp, just
slowly tightening on the sides of my temples, just
like, ahhhh.

LOTTE

I used to have a fantasy all the time about being in
a trash compactor.

PETER

Yes! That's—

LOTTE

With the walls closing in and—

PETER

Yes!

LOTTE

I'd get completely crushed, into a ball.

PETER

I think compression fantasies are quite common.
Did you ever have a hip compression thing?

LOTTE

I mean, I—

PETER

Like, when you think of yourself compressed in the
trash compactor, where are you being compressed?

LOTTE

In the centre. The trash compacting feeling is
omnidirectional. The four walls are simultaneously—

PETER

Yeah, yeah—

LOTTE

Closing in on me—

PETER

So you're being turned into a cube.

LOTTE

A cube.
(*a short pause.*)

IDA

It's different, but this reminds me of a fantasy a
friend once told me about, that every time she saw
a brick—you know, a brick by itself, not as a part
of a building—she would feel a profound desire to
smash the corner of it into her collarbone.

PETER

Hm—

LOTTE

Just the corner of it?

IDA

Just the edge of it. You know, to feel the sharp part
right on the collarbone, like / thwump—
   (*a fake karate chop on the collarbone, with her head turned.*)

LOTTE

Why the collarbone?

IDA

I don't know. I just remember how when she talked
about it, she would do this—
   (*caressing collarbone.*)
just caressing that area.
There's something perfect about the edge of a brick
smashing a collarbone. It's notoriously the most
painful bone to break.

PETER

Yeah.

LOTTE

Imagine being compelled to smash your own
collarbone—

PETER

With a brick.

                    LOTTE
Yeah.

                    PETER
Yeah. Like you were possessed.

                    LOTTE
Yeah. By a, uh...
    (*can't find word.*)

                    IDA
We used to play a game at school where we'd write
horror stories together, word by word.

                    LOTTE
Huh.

                    IDA
We'd go in a round, and each person would add a
word to the story. And you try to keep it scary.

                    LOTTE
Oh sure, that game.

                    PETER
That's a good game.

                    IDA
We should play it.

                    PETER
Now?

                    IDA
Why not?

                    LOTTE
Mm. I—

                    PETER
Alright—

                    LOTTE
Sure. I—

                    PETER
Are there any rules?

                    IDA
I don't think so. Just try to keep the story going.

                    PETER
Okay.

                    LOTTE
Alright.
    (*a short pause.*)

                    IDA
Should I start?

                    PETER
Go for it.

Another short pause, just for a second, waiting. IDA is silently choosing a single word from all of the words she knows.

                    IDA
...Christmas

                              PETER
was

                              LOTTE
coming

                    IDA
but

                              PETER
the

                              LOTTE
winter

                    IDA
was

                              PETER
long

                              LOTTE
and

                              IDA

   (*whispers.*)
harsh.

                           PETER

Peter

                           LOTTE

was

                              IDA

driving

                           PETER

his

                           LOTTE

truck

                              IDA

home

                           PETER

late

                           LOTTE

at

                              IDA

night.

	PETER
He	
	LOTTE
was	
	IDA
very	
	PETER
sleepy	
	LOTTE
on	
	IDA
his	
	PETER
...drugs	
	LOTTE
but	
	IDA
he	
	PETER
kept	
	LOTTE
driving	

	IDA
despite	
	PETER
almost	
	LOTTE
losing	
	IDA
it.	
	PETER
Then	
	LOTTE
he	
	IDA
suddenly	
	PETER
saw	
	LOTTE
through	
	IDA
the	
	PETER
...reality	

48

                    LOTTE

a

                    IDA

sad

                    PETER

hitchhiker.

                    LOTTE

So

                    IDA

brazen

                    PETER

-ly

                    LOTTE

waiting

                    IDA

beside

                    PETER

the

                    LOTTE

...fountain

                    IDA

that

                    PETER
Peter

                    LOTTE
built.

                    PETER
        (*laughing, quietly.*)
Oh, come on.

                    IDA
        (*reclaiming a serious tone.*)
The, the

                    PETER
fountain

                    LOTTE
was

                    IDA
something

                    PETER
else.

                    LOTTE
        (*after thinking for a beat.*)
The

                    IDA
hitchhiker

PETER

thumbed

LOTTE

his

IDA

...thumb

PETER

and

LOTTE

Peter

IDA

pulled

PETER

over.

LOTTE

'Do

IDA

you

PETER

want

LOTTE

to

IDA

get

PETER

in

LOTTE

my

IDA

truck?'

PETER

said

LOTTE

Peter

IDA

to

PETER

the

LOTTE

hitchhiker.

IDA

'Maybe,'

PETER

said

LOTTE

the

IDA

hitchhiker.

PETER

'What's

LOTTE

in

IDA

your

PETER

truck?'

LOTTE

Shakily,

IDA

Peter

PETER

...cowered

LOTTE

and

IDA

thought

to

LOTTE

just

IDA

...leave.

PETER

And

LOTTE

he

IDA

turned

PETER

away,

LOTTE

thinking,

IDA

'No,

PETER

that's

LOTTE

not

                    IDA

what

                    PETER

I

                    LOTTE

do.'

                    IDA

The

                    PETER

hitchhiker

                    LOTTE

yelled,

                    IDA
    (*puts hand to mouth as if speaking through a tube.*)
'Peter!

                    PETER

I

                    LOTTE

saw

                    IDA

you

PETER

think

LOTTE

about

IDA

this

PETER

night.

LOTTE

You

IDA

will

PETER

pay

LOTTE

in

IDA

blood.

PETER

Hahaha.'

LOTTE

The

                    IDA

hitchhiker

                    PETER

then

                    LOTTE

climbed

                    IDA

into

                    PETER

the

                    LOTTE

fountain

                    IDA

and

                    PETER

tore

                    LOTTE

it

                    IDA

to

                    PETER

...shreds.

LOTTE

Peter

IDA

looked

PETER

through

LOTTE

his

IDA

rearview

PETER

mirror

LOTTE

and

IDA

smiled.

PETER

'I'm

LOTTE

the

IDA

happiest

PETER

man

LOTTE

in

IDA

this

PETER

truck.'

LOTTE

'No,'

IDA

said

PETER

the

LOTTE

...corpse

IDA

in

PETER

the

LOTTE

trunk,

IDA

'I'm

PETER

the

LOTTE

happiest

IDA

man

PETER

in

LOTTE

this

IDA

truck.'

IDA leans back and looks at both PETER and LOTTE, turning her head back and forth between them with her mouth in a smile. She raises her arms above her head with her hands in fist-shapes. This signals the end of the story.

PETER

That was great! Great story.

LOTTE

Really great.

                        IDA
Great.

                        LOTTE
Really good.

                        PETER
Yeah, really good.
        (*standing up just a bit, not all the way up, but with his
        butt lifted from the seat, just about to stand all the way.*)
Uh, does anyone want anything? Water? Another beer?

                        LOTTE
Both, please.

                        IDA
Yeah, both.

PETER gets up to get the drinks, carrying the three
empty water glasses, humming a tune to himself as
he walks to the kitchen.

                        IDA
That was a pretty good story.

                        LOTTE
Yeah.

                        IDA
'I'm the happiest man...in this truck.'

                    LOTTE
Yeah.

                    IDA
Should we do another one?

                    LOTTE
     (*rubbing her eyes.*)
Ah, no...no.
     (*leans head back and stretches. bellows as if in agony.*)
No, no!

PETER, filling up glasses of water and opening beer
bottles, looks over from the kitchen. LOTTE begins
miming taking out her eyes. She pretends to dig her
fingers into her eye sockets, to get her fingers behind
her eyes, and to pull them out one by one, while making
guttural noises. As the eyes come out, she leans her head
forward slightly, as if her head is being pulled forward
by the torn-out eyes, accounting for the fact that the
eyes remain attached to the head by the optic nerve.

     it's like she has to do it. like something happened to her
     eyes and she has to get them out.
     they have to go.

After she's mimed pulling her eyes out as far the optic
nerve will allow, maybe about six inches (which is longer
than an actual optic nerve, about one and a half inches),
she makes a few final sucking noises, like shoes in mud,
that mark the end of her eye-tearing performance. She
continues holding her eyes while talking to IDA.

                              IDA
         (after a pause.)
    What are you doing?

PETER walks over and delivers the beers and then walks
back to the kitchen to get the glasses of water.

                            LOTTE
    I'm uh...uh...you know...
         (gesturing toward where the eyes are.)
    What are some words for taking out the eyes?

                              IDA
    What?

                            LOTTE
    You know, what are some words for taking out
    the eyes?

                              IDA
    Oh, um. Hm. Like, gouging?

                            LOTTE
    Yeah.

PETER walks to the centre of the kitchen. He is holding
two glasses of water in one hand, balancing them
carefully, while holding one glass in the other, taking
small sips from it, watching IDA and LOTTE talk.

                              IDA
    Scratching.

LOTTE

Thumbing.

IDA

Yeah, if thumbs are used.

LOTTE

Putting. As in, 'I'll put out your eyes.'

IDA

Plucking.

Still cradling the two glasses in one hand, PETER
stretches out his other arm and begins slowly pouring
the glass of water onto the kitchen floor, where there
is a rug. The water dribbles out at his feet and makes
the rug wet.

> *he is pouring really slowly. it's a bit of a rush at first from*
> *the glass and then it comes out of the glass in little spurts.*
> *it's running over his fingers.*
> *dripping off the bottom of his fingers.*

Neither IDA nor LOTTE respond to this action, they
just continue talking. The sound of the water dribbling
onto the rug continues. The rug is pretty wet now, so
it sounds like water hitting water, water hitting heavier
water. The pour is not fast but it's quite a heavy sound
for trickling water to make.

LOTTE

Plucking, yeah. That's like a bird doing it.

IDA

Sucking? Can eyes be sucked out?

LOTTE

Given the right, I don't know, octopus kind of thing.

IDA

But what's another word for sucking?

PETER

Pulling?

The last drops of water drip from the glass. PETER
returns to the sink, fills it back up. Then he walks back
to the sitting area with all the glasses of water. His socks
are wet. He puts the glasses of water on the coffee table
and sits back down on the couch.

LOTTE

Pulling isn't quite like sucking. Pulling is very
brutal, it's such a dull word.

IDA

Hauling?

LOTTE

Hauling it out? That implies that it's really heavy.
You can't haul a tiny gelatinous thing, can you?

PETER

No.

IDA

(*in a slightly deeper, accented voice. but no particular accent.*)

You can haul anything.

LOTTE

Popping out, you can have them popped out.

PETER

Popped out, yeah.

LOTTE

Yeah.

IDA

Ripped out, or torn out.

PETER

Teeth...are pulled out all the time—

IDA

But actually, some of these words, like ripped and torn, they don't really apply because when I think of an eye coming out, I think of it coming out whole. Not just a piece of the eye, but the whole thing somehow.

LOTTE

Yeah.

IDA

It's got to remain intact.

LOTTE

Yeah.

PETER

Hm, I—

LOTTE

What about clawed, though?

IDA

Clawed? That's good, that's close to gouged maybe.

LOTTE

But gouged makes me think of a spoon underneath
the eye,
     (*picks up a grape and holds it like an eye, mimes
     spooning it out.*)
and clawed is animalistic.
     (*makes claw.*)

IDA

Yeah, yeah, yeah.

LOTTE

What's a word for that—
     (*makes a swooshing noise.*)
—sucking out sound?

IDA

Suctioned? Suctioned out?

LOTTE

Like if you put the end of a hoover straight on your
eye and then turn it up to max—
   (*pretends to put the end of a hoover on her eye. makes a
   swooshing sound again, more watery.*)

IDA

Yeah, that would be suctioned out.

LOTTE

Maybe. Or just sucked.

IDA

Sucked.

LOTTE

Yeah.

PETER
   (*coming over to sit back down.*)
Cut!

LOTTE

Cut out. Sure, yeah.

IDA

Scooped.

LOTTE

Scooped. That's also very close to gouged.
   (*makes motion like a melon baller.*)

IDA

Dug.

LOTTE

That's like cut.

IDA

Yeah. Hooked?

LOTTE

Ow, that's awful.

PETER

Poked?

LOTTE

Kind of. But does that imply that the eyes come all
the way out?

PETER

I guess not.

(*a short pause.* IDA *notices something about* PETER.)

IDA

Are you okay?

PETER

Yeah, it's just my back. And my throat. And my head.
(*laughs a little.*)

IDA

(*sympathetically.*)
Yeah.

LOTTE picks up her beer and walks behind the couch,
stands behind PETER. She starts to massage him with
her free hand. Her hand doesn't really knead, it's more
like a sock puppet biting someone. She moves her
hand erratically from place to place on PETER, mostly
in the shouldery area and upper arm part, with a bit of
the back of the neck.

LOTTE

Okay, so we've got gouged, dug, scooped, cut,
clawed, plucked—

PETER

I like plucked, plucked is a good word.

IDA

Plucked.

LOTTE

I got a tick out last week. I plucked it out.

IDA

Really? How?

LOTTE

Just—

IDA

Were you scared?

LOTTE

Uh, so, it's interesting because first I had a dream / a
very, very visceral dream of worms being in my skin.

IDA

Huh.

LOTTE

And sort of having these raised bumps under my
skin and popping them and there being live worms
that I had to pull out.

IDA

Wow.

LOTTE

And then I woke up and realised that I had a tick
on my hip.

IDA

Wow.

LOTTE

I woke up in a haze and I was like, woah, there's
a tick on me.

IDA

(*spookily*.)
On you. Sucking your blood.

LOTTE

Yeah.

IDA

Was it upsetting?

LOTTE

It was only upsetting because I still have a mark
from it. And this was a week and a half ago.

IDA

You managed to get its face out, though?

LOTTE

Yeah.

IDA

How are you sure?

LOTTE

Well, I just...
    (*makes pinching motions with fingers.*)

PETER

With your fingers?

IDA

But you're sure you took it out the right way? You
got its face out?

                    LOTTE
I have long fingernails.
    (*looks at her fingernails.*)

                     IDA
I have fingernails too. But I don't think I'd trust
myself to get the face out.

                    LOTTE
Well, you just go deep and then make sure its head
is there / look at it closely...
    (*looks at pinched fingers where the tick is/would be.*)

                     IDA
Yeah, but that's quite hard. Afterwards you can
confirm, but it's quite hard to see what you're doing
while you're doing it.

                    LOTTE
Well, if I saw the head was lodged in there I probably
would have gone to the doctor.

                     IDA
Yeah, sure.

                    PETER
Yeah.

                    LOTTE
My sister asked me if I put it in a little vial and took
it to the hospital.

                    IDA
Why?

                    PETER
To test it?

                    LOTTE
Yeah.

                    IDA
For lyme disease?

                    LOTTE
Yeah.

                    IDA
Oh, come on.

                    PETER
I bet if you brought a bug in a vial to a hospital,
they'd just tell you to leave.

                    IDA
        (*in her funny lower voice.*)
'Go home.'

                    PETER
        (*wincing a little from the massage.*)
Yeah.

LOTTE stops her hand from massaging PETER more.
She pats him on the shoulder as if to let him know

he's done getting a massage. She takes a swig from her beer as she walks back to her seat on purpose. There is a short pause in the conversation. IDA talks next.

                    IDA
You were talking about dreaming about worms under your skin, well, maybe your sister also told you that I had surgery earlier this week?

                  LOTTE
Yeah.

                  PETER
Mmm—

                    IDA
It's okay, it's not a secret.
      (*waves her hand.*)

                  PETER
Are you—

                    IDA
Well, um, apart from the fact that the whole thing was sad and gross—well, not gross actually, but you know—but apart from that, the scariest part was having general anaesthetic, because I never had general anaesthetic before.

                  LOTTE
Oh wow.

PETER

Yeah.

IDA

I did not take it well. I was crying because I was worried that I was going to die. The nurses asked me, 'Do you have any questions?' And I was like, 'Am I going to die?'

LOTTE

Yeah.

IDA

It's a risk, right? You can't say it's not a risk because it is a risk.

LOTTE

Yeah.

IDA

I told them, 'Tell me it's a risk. I have a child I have to go home to. I need to know if I'm going to die.'

LOTTE

Yeah—

PETER

Yeah.

IDA

They were like, 'You're not going to die, you're not like 90 with preexisting health conditions. Come

on, you're not going to fucking die!' And I was like,
'Okay, fine, thank you.'

PETER

Yeah. Good answer. They're right.

IDA

Then they put the, you know—
    (*makes motion, presses with two fingers into back of hand.*)
in my hand.

LOTTE

The what in your hand?

PETER

The IV.

IDA

The straw. The straw. They put a needle in your
hand but then they pull the needle out so the straw
stays in your hand. So they can pump in whatever
they want.
    (*makes gesture like sweeping something off the top of
    her hand.*)

PETER

Oh yeah. I've had that.

IDA

Yeah.

PETER

But your fears are understandable. I mean, it's just
general anaesthetic, but still, there's always a chance…

IDA

Yeah, exactly.

PETER

There are so many things like that, where one in
a million people have some fatal reaction. Like to
antibiotics or something.

IDA

The anaesthetic thing is different, it's like one in
30,000.

LOTTE

That someone dies?

IDA

Yeah!

LOTTE

One in 30,000? No.

PETER

(*to* IDA)
I bet it will be you.
(*pause.*)
I bet it will be you.

LOTTE sniffs or inhales. IDA looks at PETER, PETER'S face, then turns to LOTTE and leans in.

                              IDA
It reminds me of what I told you about blue tits.

                            LOTTE
Oh, I've been thinking about this.

                            PETER
What?

                            LOTTE
I was just thinking about this yesterday.

                            PETER
    (*a little whiny.*)
Thinking about what?

                            LOTTE
Last week she told me that she was listening to a
radio programme called 'Numbers that You Won't
Believe.' And it was about these certain chicks of
a common bird...

                              IDA
Blue tits—

                            LOTTE
Yeah, blue tits. And the number that you won't believe
was that one chick will eat 35 billion caterpillars a year.

PETER

That can't be true.
   (*coughs a little.*)

LOTTE

Yeah, and I was like, 'You're right, I don't believe that!'
And she was like, 'No, it's true, it was on the programme!'

IDA

It was!

LOTTE

And I went through the numbers in my head yesterday
as I was biking to work, and I figured out that if one
chick ate 35 billion caterpillars in a year, it would have
to eat a thousand every second.
   (PETER *cough-laughs.*)
It would have to hammer its head at like 60,000 RPM.
Like—
   (*shouting while jabbing downwards with her forefinger).*
blllllllll!!
   (PETER *coughs into his elbow. hard enough to*
   interrupt.)
Concert A—
   (PETER *continues coughing.*)
—Are you okay?
   (PETER *waves his hand like he's telling her to continue*
   talking with his hand.)
Concert A on a piano is 440 Hz, so it would have to
be way over an octave—
   (PETER *is still coughing really hard. a little harder.*)

PETER
(*stops coughing. sits up. watery eyes. grimace type of thing. leans back, swallows.*)
Sorry. I think I must have bronchitis or something.

IDA
(*pats and strokes the top of the couch tenderly in time with her words.*)
I think if you had bronchitis you'd be coughing a lot more often.

PETER
Yeah, yeah, you're right.

(*a medium-long pause in which* LOTTE *looks down and then up.*)

LOTTE
Do you want us to go?

IDA
Yeah, I should get home soon anyway.

PETER
You don't have to...

IDA
No, I should make a move.

LOTTE
Yeah. I think it's time.

(IDA *and* LOTTE *simultaneously scoot and lean forward in their chairs and drink the last bits they want from their beers.*)

PETER

Well...

(IDA *and* LOTTE *simultaneously half-stand. they are standing but they are still bent at the waist in a sitting position, hovering over the table as if they are about to help clear the table.*)

LOTTE

Should we...?

PETER

No, no, no...

IDA

Thanks for...

PETER

Yeah, of course...

LOTTE

Yeah, thanks for...

IDA and LOTTE stand. IDA reaches down and takes one last grape, yoink, and pops it in her mouth. They walk to the door and begin taking their hats and coats down from the hatstand. They are quiet as they put their arms in their coats, heads in their hats.

                              IDA
So nice to see you.

                             PETER
Yeah, it really was.

                             LOTTE
Lovely to see you both.

                             PETER
So lovely.

                              IDA
Yeah.

        (IDA *and* PETER *hug goodbye. Then* LOTTE *and*
        PETER *hug goodbye.*)

                             LOTTE
Feel better.

                             PETER
Yeah.

                              IDA
Bye.

                             PETER
Bye.
        (*holds the door open as they go out.*)

PETER closes the door slowly and then stands there for a moment.

He touches his throat with his index and middle finger, feeling for swollen lymph nodes. Other than that, he shows no signs of sickness.

He walks across the room and turns off a lamp. He immediately turns it back on.

> *walks over to the TV remote, uses it to turn on the TV.*
> *the sound is all the way up and it blurts very loud.*
> *way too loud.*
> *hits the mute button a few times before the TV listens and mutes.*

PETER watches the TV for a few seconds, then walks across the room to the kitchen, over to the kettle. He fills it up in the sink, puts it back on the little plastic bottom-thing that heats it up, and turns it on.

While he waits for it to boil, he walks over to the armchair and sits. He sits low in the chair, with his arms on the armrests.

For a few moments, PETER half-watches what's on TV. After a bit, while still facing the TV, he reaches behind him in a stiff backstroke to pat the top of the radiator that's behind him. Then he returns his arm to where it was on the armrest and sits in that pose for a moment. Suddenly, PETER turns all the way around, as if he's made a decision to do so. He turns and kneels up on

the seat and leans over the back of the chair like a dog
on a chair, so that his neck is pressed against the top
of the back of the chair as he peers into the radiator.
He reaches down and pats the underneath of the radiator.
His hand is in a rigid scoop shape while he pats. There's
no flexibility in the forearm or wrist.

> *when the kettle pops, he jumps up.*
> *like he is almost excited about it and walks toward the*
> *kitchen like he is almost jogging toward the kitchen. on*
> *the way to the kitchen, when passing the table, he pauses,*
> *looks at the table really quickly and then lies on it,*
> *presses his torso against the table.*
> *hugs the table and uses his hands to steady himself by*
> *hooking them under the sides of the table.*
> *stiffens his legs and bends them at the knee so his feet are*
> *up and pointed like a ballet dancer's feet, crossed at the*
> *ankles. his whole body is stiffened.*

> 'Stiffening' is a kind of semi-conscious/
> compulsive self-pleasuring where every muscle
> in the body is tensed for a short period.

> *tenses every muscle in his body. his breath is shallow,*
> *staccato, and wobbles a little with the effort. he stiffens*
> *for thirty seconds or so. then he relaxes and gets off the*
> *table and continues to the kitchen.*

In the kitchen, PETER reaches into a cupboard and
removes a resealable plastic bag with powder in it, then
spoons out maybe one and a half scoops into a mug.

He pours hot water into the mug and stirs in the powder while walking back to the living room area.

As he's walking back to the living room area, he pauses,

> *pulls the spoon out, taps it on the rim of the mug to knock the liquid off, blows on it a bit, then puts it in his mouth to get the rest of the liquid off, then turns and tosses the spoon back into the sink.*
> *it's a perfect throw, lands in the sink.*

The spoon makes a loud clang in the sink.

He continues walking back to the living room area but stops and turns to face the TV. He bends over the drink and sips very cautiously because the water is very hot.

> *like he's inhaling the top skin of the drink.*
> *breathing/sucking over the surface until a tiny bit of drink shoots in and it's hot so he stops immediately.*

He straightens up and waits a moment. Then he bends over the drink again (hunching at the shoulders) and this time he whistles just slightly, like wind, as he blows to cool the surface of the drink and moves to suck it up.

Once more he straightens back up and waits. He turns to the TV. Then back to the drink. He bends down one more time to suck at it, hot!, and when he straightens up he turns to the radiator at the front of the room and bends right down to feel the underside to see how hot it is. Though his body is bent almost in half, at the waist, the arm with the mug remains at the same elevation as it was when he was up straight, so he doesn't spill anything.

PETER straightens up again and fiddles with the knob of the radiator. He turns it one way and then back to where it was.

PETER mooches across to another radiator and runs his fingers lightly over the top of it as he walks past. He's holding the mug up to his mouth like a microphone. At the end of the radiator, he turns around and walks back to the centre of the room, where he notices a speck on the floor and gracefully bends down to wipe it up with his index fingertip. When he bends, he raises one leg behind him in a swoop, like a dog pissing or a swan's neck arching.

> *straightens up again.*
> *walks over to the coffee table. looms over it, looking at the empty beer bottles left there.*

PETER pushes a pinky finger into the mouth/neck of a bottle, then his ring finger into another, then his middle finger into a third, then his index finger into one more bottle, and lifts all the bottles at once so they are dangling from his hand like a chandelier/wind chimes/ really big noisy glove. Hunched and shuffling slowly and carefully so as not to drop them, he carries them toward the sink.

he's still holding the mug all this time.
still holding the mug.

On the way to the sink, PETER uses his crotch to nudge
the dining chairs closer to the table.

He puts the mug down on the kitchen counter. Then he
puts the bottles into the sink.

extracts his fingers one by one and then upends the bottles
all at once, emptying the dregs into the sink. then takes
them to beside the pedal bin, puts them on the floor.
back to the sink.
runs a cloth under the tap and wrings the cloth out.

PETER moves over to the dining table. The surface is
lightly cluttered. There's a thermos, an open laptop,
a set of keys, and a printer cartridge. PETER just starts
wiping the table.

When he comes to the thermos, he lifts it with one hand
while wiping underneath with the other. Same with
the open laptop. PETER picks it up by the top of the
screen, between two fingers. He wipes underneath and
then puts it down in the same spot.

When PETER comes to the keys, he bats them around
like a cat toying with an insect, pushing them out of
the way of where he wants to wipe.

But when PETER gets to the part of the table with the
printer cartridge, he doesn't lift it or move it out of

the way—he just wipes the cloth toward it without hesitation. It lifts on its own: just as the cloth reaches it, the printer cartridge rises from the table and levitates a few inches in the air, enough for PETER'S hand to pass under it easily. It floats there, motionless, completely at rest, hanging in the air. It doesn't descend again. It will never come back down.

    the printer cartridge is floating there forever.

PETER tosses the cloth into the sink, like he did with the spoon, and it also lands in the sink, like the spoon did.

PETER goes to the counter and picks up the plastic box that the grapes came in. It's a bulky rectangular shape. He opens the pedal bin with his foot and pushes the plastic thing into the rather full garbage bag. He continues pushing it down slowly and steadily so that his entire arm disappears into the bin. His head is cocked as he does this, looking down. It's like there's a wire attached to his head that's on a spool at the bottom of the bin and PETER is being reeled in. The packaging makes a plasticky crinkling sound as it's crushed.

PETER pauses, his arm in the bin. Then he pulls his arm out.

He pulls the garbage bag out and sits it on the counter. He finds the thin plastic ribbon in the waistband of the bag and teases out either end of the ribbon so that the waistband tightens. He ties it off and carries the bag in one hand over to the front door.

PETER picks up a shoe that's sitting by the door.

> *still holding the bin bag in his right hand.*
> *pulling the tongue forward and opening up the mouth*
> *of the shoe, his leg is lifted in a sideways pyramid shape*
> *so that his heel is near his other knee (is there a ballet*
> *name for this?). he slips the shoe onto his foot and*
> *stomps to the ground with the full weight of his foot*
> *plus his leg.*
> *then he does the same with the other foot/shoe, and*
> *stumbles when he stomps down, lurches an extra step.*

PETER walks out through the front door with the bag, leaving it ajar.

The room is empty. The lights are a bit brighter without PETER in the room. The radiators hiss. The bed continues to writhe. The TV is still on. The whole space is louder. The room is filling. It sounds like everything is losing air,

> *as if the couch is collapsing,*

> *the table is shrinking,*

> *the lamps are dimming,*

> *the chairs are flattening,*

> *the kitchen cabinets are sinking into a lumpy mass and*
> *all the plates and glasses are about to fall off and shatter.*

It also sounds as if everything is being pumped full of air,

as if the couch is ballooning out into a blimpy shape,

the coffee table is puffing up,

the chairs are rounding,

the whole kitchen is looking more like a ball,

the refrigerator is swelling and its door is about to burst open and the food inside is about to spill all over the floor.

After a minute or so, PETER walks back in, he doesn't have the bag.

He closes the door quietly. He squats and takes off his shoes. He's back in socks.

When he stands again, he pauses to listen. He hears a sound coming from the neighbours' apartment and walks over to put his ear against a wall and listen. He has a little smile on his face like he is thinking 'Oh, those fucking neighbours and their noises.' The sound does not happen again.

PETER walks to the coffee table with small steps (his feet don't lift much) in a straight line like he's on a track to the coffee table. His body doesn't change as he walks and he's looking ahead at where he's going.

He picks up the remote and changes the channel, then changes it back. Then he goes and sits on the middle of the couch and puts his arm on the back of the couch, facing the TV.

PETER looks at his hand on the back of the couch. He raises his hand in a 'halt' gesture as if to examine his fingernails, then turns his hand the other way and curls his fingers toward his palm as if to examine his fingernails, then turns back to the 'halt' gesture.

> *tenderly strokes the top of the couch with that hand, the right hand.*
> *back and forth.*
> *does that a few times, and while watching that hand, he slips his other hand, the left hand, without looking at it, into the crevice between the seat cushions to his left and pushes down into the couch, slowly and deliberately.*
> *continuing to watch the same hand he has been watching, the right hand, he slides this hand down and inserts it into the crevice between the seat cushions to his right.*
> *he holds his hands flat and hard, like flippers.*

He sits straight up, still looking to his right, at the TV, with his hands stuffed into the couch up to his wrists.

Raising his shoulders slightly, like he was hunching in the cold, he uses his shoulders to pump his arms up and down slowly, so that his hands move a little in and out of the cushions, not completely, such that he presumably feels the tightness of the cushions around his flippers.

maybe four times.

Then he pauses, as if he's a machine that's been turned off, looks at nothing. Suddenly, he arches his back, lifting his ass from the couch, tensing every muscle as he did when stiffening on the table, and holds himself up in a spidery pose.

he is balanced on the following points: his toes on the floor, his hands in the couch.
his hips are thrust up, like he was being picked up by the crotch.
his head is leaned back over the top of the couch, staring at the ceiling.
his face is turning red with the strain of holding his whole body taut. he wobbles with the strain.
he's holding his breath.
his chest is puffed-out like a pigeon's chest.

He holds this stiffening pose for 25 seconds or so, then, as if whatever was holding him by the crotch releases him, he drops his ass back into the couch and sits up straight again, for less than a second or so, before he topples over sideways and faceplants into the couch.

His feet are flat on the floor.

PETER finally takes a big breath, sucking in air. He drags his right hand across his legs, like he was tracing a mountain range—there's something topographical about this movement—to where his head lies and lifts the couch cushion beneath his head so that the couch opens, like he was opening the couch's mouth, or like he was hiding his face with the cushion. He holds the couch mouth open for five seconds or so. Then he closes it, pushes himself back up, and sits upright.

His hands are no longer in the crevices. They are just sitting there.

He pats the couch, as if patting it is a kind of tidying.

PETER then gets up and walks over to the fridge. He walks like a cowboy, moseying. Legs and arms are a bit stiff, maybe from the workout on the couch.

He squats in front of the fridge with a grunt, teeters on the balls of his feet while squatting, pulling things out to get to something that's in the back. He pulls out a number of pieces of tupperware, filled with presumably leftovers, and lines them up quite carefully on the floor. Also a plastic tub of hummus. He seems to know the general area in the fridge where whatever he's looking for is, and he's pulling things out to better access that area.

PETER pulls out some tupperware with spaghetti in it and reaches up and plonks it on top of the fridge.

> he carefully puts the other tupperwares back in the
> fridge, sometimes using one tupperware to push another
> tupperware deeper into the depths of the fridge. all the

tupperwares go back into the fridge except for the one on
the top of the fridge with the spaghetti in it.
when he puts the hummus back, he opens it and trails a
finger through, then sucks it off his finger.
closes the fridge.

Then PETER closes the fridge, gets a fork out of a drawer,
takes the tupperware from the top of the fridge, opens
it, and starts walking while using the fork to toss the
cold spaghetti like a salad, loosening it up, getting it
ready for eating.

Looking down at the spaghetti, he slowly twirls a forkful
around the fork. There's a lot of spaghetti on the fork.
As he coaxes the spaghetti out of the tupperware, he
assesses the huge amount. It trails, pulling, pulling
a whole wig of spaghetti behind it when he lifts the
fork. He lowers his head to meet the fork and puts the
spaghetti in his mouth with a clang (the sound of the
fork on his teeth) and, in short gaspy inhalations, he
sucks in the spaghetti without cutting it off with his
teeth, until the bundle of spaghetti is all inside him,
which takes about 11 seconds, at which point he sighs
audibly through his nose, without opening his mouth,
like a satisfied cartoon bear.

He starts wandering around the perimeter of the
apartment with the pasta, frequently looking down
at the pasta while he chews. In front of the TV, he stops
again, without looking at the TV, and bows his head
to the pasta again, eating another oversized forkful.
As he sucks in the spaghetti, the last few inches of the

spaghetti wriggle like they don't want to be eaten, like a mouse's tail being eaten by a cartoon cat. He sighs again, deeply.

While he's chewing this mouthful, he walks around the couch, around the coffee table, past the TV, and around to the front door, where he eats another large mouthful of spaghetti.

PETER begins wandering back to the kitchen area, toying with the pasta, mixing it around with his fork, chewing. As he passes the massive screen/mirror at the back of the room, his image appears on the screen and he freezes for a moment, mid-forkful, looking at himself and tilting his head as if he's had an idea for something he could do in front of this massive screen/mirror.

He walks away, stirs the pasta once more, half-assedly, and puts the tupperware on the table.

> *grabs the nearest chair from the dining table and drags it on its back legs toward the table where the screen/mirror is.*
> *the table is like a kind of dressing table, low-ish like a child's desk or at least like a small teenager's desk. there's nothing on it and it's black. there's a cutout on the top and there's a camera sticking out, pointed upward at where* PETER'S *head would be when he is sitting in the chair. there is a projector making quite a lot of noise in a box in the table!*
> *whatever the camera sees is what is projected on the screen,*

like a mirror. in this case, PETER'S head.
his head is very large-sized on the screen/mirror, filling it
up with his face.
there are lights embedded in the table as well, aimed at
his face.

PETER sits before the mirror and looks. The lights
in the room dim and the lights in the table brighten.
The projection of PETER's face is vivid.

He looks at himself without examining himself, not like
he is checking out a mole or scrutinising a new wrinkle,
just looking at his face. He moves his head a bit, maybe
he fishes the last bit of spaghetti out of his teeth with
his tongue. This is all a pause.

After the pause, with one hand, PETER reaches up and
matter-of-factly pretends to unscrew and remove an
eye, making convincing squishy noises with his mouth.
The eye pops out and he makes a little popping sound
with his mouth, and he pretends to look at the removed
eye with his other eye.

PETER takes the unscrewed eye and pretends to put it on
the tabletop, all the way to the left. Then he continues
to mime unpacking his face, removing his features one
by one and placing them on the table.

He doesn't necessarily do all of the following actions,
and not necessarily in this order. Maybe half. He
proceeds with a straightforwardness, like he has done
this before, pretending to remove the features of his

97

face. He places each feature on the table in a line that extends from left to right. He pauses between each action, as if to let his face reset. The whole routine takes about 10 minutes.

POP EYE OUT. With one hand, stretch lids, with the other take the eye out, like taking out a contact but the whole eye. Slight shiver. The body doesn't necessarily want to do it. Like when you're trying to make yourself sick, there's some resistance in the body. Hold it preciously, like if you were taking apart a watch or a clock. Don't lose the little bits. It comes away with a little gunk, catch that gunk as well. Maybe a string follows the eye. Be careful with it. Look at it, check that it's all there.

TEETH. Just a few at a time, using fingers like pliers, and then maybe take out the whole bottom layer at once, like dentures. Teeth are quite hard, so you need to use both hands. Some are more stubborn than others. Strain against them and then they give, come out in a rush. Tonguing of the gum where the tooth was. It's bloody.

PEELING OFF LIPS. Like getting your fingernail under tape, hard to catch the edge. Slow. Be careful not to snap it, break it. Both lips in one motion.

NOSE. Quick snap and then pull off with a catching motion. Hold it delicately in two hands as it's placed on the table.

EARS. Peel them down. They come right off.

CHEEK. Puff it up. Get the skin at the base of the jaw. As if there's a zip. Finding it is a bit hard, once you've got the zip hold the cheek so it doesn't drop on the floor, but unzip with relief. Relaxing of the face. Only one cheek.

FIND CENTRAL ZIPPER IN HAIR. Rooting around in hair on the back of the head. Find it, unzip it to chin or bottom of neck. Pull apart from the forehead. When it's unzipped, it's baggy. Then it's kind of on your shoulders, brush it back like a hood. This one doesn't go on the table. You just wear it, like a hood.

EYES AGAIN. Hand in front, ready to catch the eye. Thwack at the back of the head, the eye falls into the hand. One and then the other.

JAW. Move it back and forth to loosen it a bit. Side to side. Then pull out of socket. Not too much resistance. Like pulling the limb of a plastic figurine and it pops out of the ball joint.

TONGUE. Some pulling with both hands with fingers on the sides of the tip, and then a (gentle?) yank. It comes out pretty easily. Hold it very delicately. Tongues are quite long, longer than you would think. You have to drape it down slightly.

FISTFUL OF HAIR. Kind of like pulling hair out of a hairbrush, getting a clump and pulling it at once.

THROAT. Small door on neck. Little handle that you turn, or a catch. Open the door as if it's a closet, it swings open. One hand has to hold the door open (it's a little heavy) while the other hand gets in there. Remove something from the neck with a few fingers, like you're taking a doll's dress on a hanger off a rack in a dollhouse. Then close the door. You don't want to leave that open.

AIR AROUND THE EYES. The area that would be under goggles. Basically looks like you are taking off goggles, but there's no band holding them on. Not actually goggles. Like air that is somehow suctioned to the face.

BRIDGE OF NOSE. Pulling it out. Doesn't resist at all. Like it's just sitting there on top of the nose, balanced there.

AIR AROUND THE CHEEKS.

FIND SOMETHING, LITTLE BITS, BETWEEN LIPS AND GUMS. Way up in there. Unscrew it. Or unplug it. Like finding a tiny screw when you don't have the right tool and you try to do it with your fingers.

TOUCH ROOF OF MOUTH, JUST BEFORE THE GAGGING POINT. So there's a little bit of a hesitation because you don't want to gag. As if pressing a button, like a reset button that's on the back of a machine, in a place where it's not easy for it to be accidentally pressed. You have to press quite hard. But it doesn't do anything that we can see. Pull finger out slowly.

HAND UNDER CHIN. Scoop it up and peel face off. Rubber mask sort of thing.

FEELING OUT THE TIP OF THE NOSE, LOOKING FOR SOMETHING THAT'S HIDDEN FROM VIEW. Touching the tip of the nose, moving it from one side to the other gently, stretching the nostrils, as if looking for something. Slight catch (looking inwards), concentrating through the tip of the finger. Then you find it.

PULLING OUT A LONG ROPE OUT OF A CHEEK.

PEELING THROAT DOWN FROM JOWLS. Make a ridge of flesh to grab (by pinching). Get that with your fingers and then pull it forwards, down. Like a bib. Maybe move head a little so the bib of the neck flops down in the right position, not too chickeny.

PULLING OFF HUNKS OF FLESH FROM CHEEKS AND NECK (ALSO BACK OF NECK). You have to scrunch it up like balls of it before you pull it off in a handful, maybe it's slightly disgusting, drop it on the table, make a mound of it. Don't treat it too preciously. Some of these things are treated very delicately, but you can get hunks of flesh anywhere, they are common, and they are not so fragile.

TAKING OUT A MOLAR. One hand holds the mouth open, the other reaches in for the molar. Hold it open like you would a crocodile's mouth, or a manhole cover, or a heavy wooden lid to an old chest— something where if you let go it would slam shut. And you don't want it to do that because your hand is in there getting the molar out. Pulling it out with the thumb and forefinger. Jiggle it a bit, but it's coming away a little too easily.

TAKING OFF HELMET, LIKE AN ASTRONAUT'S HELMET. Slight twist to free it. Wait a second as the air rushes out. Or in.

PULL OFF A SPECK OF SOMETHING AS IF IT WAS A MOLE OR A TICK, SOMETHING SMALL, ON THE NECK. You are almost completely static, working away at it with tiny movements. You can't see what your fingers are doing, even in the mirror. This takes slightly longer, it's very concentrated work.

EYELASHES, ONE BY ONE (ON ONE EYE). Fingers as tweezers, plucking them. A sharp plucking motion.

It seems like PETER always ends this routine with the head, like the head is an obvious ending point. Before taking his head off, he steels himself, takes a few breaths.

places one hand on the back of his head and one hand
under the chin.
takes a moment to be sure that his hands are in the right
place, that he can do it with the proper torque.

TAKING OFF HEAD. Sudden twist, it comes off
with a little pop. Similar twist to the helmet. Handle
it very carefully, like putting down an expensive
fragile vase. Very carefully. Adjust it when it's on
the table. Like you are turning it to face you.

PETER is done with this game. He has a slight smile
on his face and his eyes are wet. He pretends to sweep
everything on the table off the table, onto the floor,
with his hands.

He brushes off the surface of the table, polishing it a
little with his sleeve. He stands up and walks away from
the screen/mirror.

the lights in the room brighten again.
picks up the tupperware from the dining table with some
residual spaghetti in it and drops it into the sink with
a clunk.
walks purposefully and a little fast toward the door, as
if he's heading to the door, but halfway there he turns
around and walks back toward the dining table again.

When he gets to the dining table, PETER squats behind
it, squatting with a very straight back, facing the fridge.
Then he rotates on the balls of his feet and faces the
door again. He grabs the nearest table leg with one hand

and puts the fingertips of the other hand on the lip of the table. His cheek is resting against the lip of the table. It looks like he's hiding behind the table or pretending that his head is an object sitting on the table.

The lights go out, the TV goes off, the screen/mirror goes off, and the room is dark.

Appendices

Plumbing

The walls of the apartment are described by the plumbing. There are three cast-iron free-standing steam radiators: two at the front of the stage and one stage left, next to the living room area. Pipes connect these radiators and go around the whole apartment, they are raised a couple of inches from the floor with saddle clips. At the kitchen area, the pipes climb up and trace the top of the cupboards. At the screen/mirror (see APPENDIX D), they run along the floor. At the door, they scoot around the doorframe.

IMPORTANT: The radiators are plumbed into the central heating of the theatre. They are on and quite warm. The sink is also plumbed in and works.

> *the audience might not ever or might never notice that the radiators are real.*
> *there is nothing that signals their functionality other than the fact that they are warm. also, there is the moment that* PETER *leans in to adjust one of the radiators and his microphone picks up the sound of water moving in it.*

Sound

There are a lot of microphones on stage. Each actor wears a lavalier mic taped to their face. There are contact microphones hidden in the furniture in the living room area and in the kitchen area. There are 30 or so contact mics under the floor.

Throughout the play, there is a sound bed of room tone. This was recorded in the same room (ED'S living room) as the conversations that were transcribed and edited to build the dialogue in the first half.

All sounds are mono and lumped together. The room tone mixes with the stage tone. At all times, there is the hiss of everything.

> *couch crinkles.*
> *the floor has squeaks and squelches. the floor is raised to fit the contact mics in.*
> *the mics on the actors are really high. pretty much as high as they can go without feeding back. the actors don't need to project their voices because of the mics, they can speak low. when* IDA *eats the grapes, the grape sound is good and loud, squishy.*
> *the actors' mics are picking up other sounds on their lavalier mics (couch, fridge, slurps, radiator, projector, bin).*

> *when* PETER *takes the trash out, the room tone and all the mics are cut for one minute. silence until he comes back.*

there is one instance of non-diegetic sound, when
the neighbours make a sound after PETER *returns*
from taking the trash out. this is a sound effect:
Bodyfall_carpet_11.wav pushed through a low-pass filter.

PETER *does his own face foley. he uses his mouth to*
soundtrack his actions while he unpacks his face. it's
a bit gratuitous and gory-sounding.

Levitation

First thing: take an HP 410A LaserJet toner cartridge (or something similar-looking), empty out the toner, and then reweight it so the weight is evenly distributed.

When the printer cartridge levitates, it is being lifted with a pulley by an invisible thread, the kind that magicians use. The pulley is operated by the stage manager.

To steady the cartridge, four invisible threads are attached to the table where the four corners of the cartridge sit, but they are not attached to the cartridge. Instead, there are four holes drilled through the cartridge at those points and the threads run through those holes. These threads do not lift the cartridge, but they stabilise it so that it does not wobble too much in the air.

There is one thread attached to the middle of the cartridge. This is the only thread that does the lifting.

The lifting thread is actually made of four segments of differing thicknesses. Because the lower part is in the area of the stage that is well-lit, it must be very thin. The next length, a little higher, where the lighting is lower, is a bit thicker, to strengthen it. These first two are both made of magicians' invisible thread. Then there is a segment of elastic, so that the lifting has a certain grace. Finally, the elastic is tied to rope, which is the part that goes over the pulley.

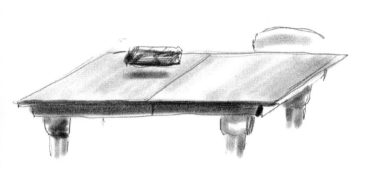

Screen/mirror

A screen/mirror thing is at the centre of the back of the
stage. It's about two metres square.

In front of the screen/mirror is a low table/counter thing,
the same length as the mirror and at the height of a desk.
It's quite deep. Why? Well, it's deep enough to allow
for a rectangular hole to be cut out of it to fit a projector
that is suspended in a wooden box beneath the table/
counter thing. Because the projector is so close to the
screen/mirror, the projector has an ultra-short-throw
periscopic lens on it.

Beneath the screen/mirror is a camera on a tripod with
a lens with a very low aperture and a strong zoom, so
that when something comes close to it, it is very clear,
and when things are more distant, they are abstract
and blobby. This camera is angled up at the face of
whoever (PETER) sits at the table/counter thing. The
camera feeds the projector this image. The projector
projects this image onto the screen/mirror.

> *for most of the play, the audience cannot see anything in
> particular on the screen/mirror, it's kind of like a
> splotchy grey light.*
> *when the actors pass by on their way, they suddenly and
> briefly show up on the screen/mirror.*
> *when* PETER *sits down to unpack his face, two lights by
> the camera shine up to light up his face. at the same*

*exact time, the stage lights dim, except for the lights on
the* PETER *area.*
when PETER *is there, all the focus is on the screen/
mirror—except that the TV is still on all this time
(*SEE APPENDIX G*), so there are actually two screens
on stage to look at.*

Theme tune

The theme tune is played as the audience is entering and waiting for the play to begin, and again right after the play is over, as they are leaving.

It is a recording of a malfunctioning smooth jazz radio station. It is mostly hissy silence, and then blurts of half-seconds of music at regular intervals.

Two People Attempting to Place a Penknife on a Bed
so that It Appears as if No One Put It There

> *as we were beginning to work on* Sorcerer, *we wrote a*
> *number of short things to test out some ideas.*
> *one of these things was a conversation and game we did*
> *between us about how to place a penknife on a bed so*
> *that it appears as if no one put it there.*
> *we played this game for a while at* STEVE'S *apartment*
> *in a room with a bed in it, then recorded and transcribed*
> *it. there was editing involved afterward.*

So, I suppose we should first eliminate places where it
would be really obvious that someone put it there, like
a chocolate-on-a-pillow kind of thing.

Yeah, that's right. That would look very intentional.

And maybe dead centre would also be too much, even
though there would be an uncanniness to that. But it
would be too—

If it was dead centre then I don't think it should be
parallel to any right angle. Do you know what I mean?
It should be slightly off.

Yeah, but that's not enough. I think it shouldn't be
in the centre at all, no matter if it's slightly skewed.

Okay, so let's rule out the centre.

Yeah.

What about the bottom corner?

Well, now it looks like an object that's...gathered at the bottom of the bed.

What do you mean?

Like if you take off your socks in bed and then they get kicked to the bottom. You know? It's just easy to imagine how it got there.

Oh, yeah. True.

Well, maybe let's try tossing it on the bed and seeing what happens.

Good idea. Should the knife be open or closed?

I think open.

Open. Fully? Because fully open is very aggressive, it's quite threatening. If someone sees it, they're much more likely to think, 'Fuck, this is a knife.'

Yeah, yeah, yeah. But partway open is aggressive in a different way. It suggests the knife is about to be opened.

No, then it just looks unused. You can't do anything with

a half-open knife. It doesn't work as a weapon.

Hm. I'm not sure about that. But okay, let's just leave it fully open. That's more neutral, because maybe leaving it partway open implies that it was left behind in the middle of an action. All the way open doesn't necessarily imply any action.

Yeah, good point.

Do you want to try throwing it onto the bed, or are you going to pass by and drop it?

I'm going to throw it high.

Okay, good idea.

Here it goes...

(*throws the penknife high in the air, it lands on the bed.*)

Oh, that's really nice. I like where it landed.

Yeah, it fell nicely inside of a—

A fold of the duvet.

Yeah. That's interesting. But we don't want to hide the knife. If it's hidden, it suggests that someone did the hiding.

Yeah.

What if we make it very conspicuous?

How so?

Like, what if it was standing on its end? Would that help, or not?

I don't know, give it a shot.

Okay...

   (*tries to stand the penknife on its end. it keeps falling over.*)

Hm...

This isn't working. I don't think I can do it.

It seems pretty hard to do.

Yeah. It will only stand up if we lean it against the pillow like this.

   (*leans the penknife against a pillow.*)

It looks like it's sleeping, propped on the pillow.

That's too cute. What if, instead, we prop it up on the folds of the duvet?

   (*props the penknife on the folds of the duvet.*)

Good idea.

That looks good.

Yeah, and if we twist the folds (*twists folds*)...it looks like something that's in the process of being revealed, or maybe something that was just revealed.

Yeah, and the creases in the duvet really help, because it almost looks like the knife is about to float down a little riverbed or something...

A gully, yeah.

Yeah, a gully.

And the knife is not completely hidden by the folds but it's not the first thing you would see, either.

Not at all.

That looks good.

Yes. It looks like it's rising up to meet the day, like it's getting out of bed. Or like it wants to leap over to the pillow. It feels quite optimistic. Even positive.

Yeah, it's a positively charged scene.

And a knife on a bed, even if it's a penknife, is nine times out of ten going to be quite upsetting, I think.

And this does not look that upsetting.

Yeah, no. I almost think you wouldn't notice it, mainly because it's not being aggressive at all, really.

Yeah, I think that's right.

It looks very...dainty, in fact.

Yeah. It's really nice.

Is it too nice? Does it look too neatly arranged?

That's a good question. Maybe. Hm.

What if we just twisted the duvet a little (*twists duvet*)... like this (*continues twisting*)...so that it covers the knife a bit more. Does that make it less nice?

Huh. Now it looks like it fell into a little hole...no, wrong word, uh...

A divot.

A divot, yeah. It fell into a divot.

It looks trapped now, doesn't it?

Yeah.

Or like it's being held by the duvet. Embraced.

That's not bad.

No, it's not bad.

It's not bad. But it's a bit too...um...orderly. It looks like someone dug a little hole in the duvet and then dropped the knife in.

Into the divot.

Yeah.

I think we should move on. I'm going to try throwing it again.

The last time we threw it, it did something good.

Yeah, the throwing helps.

It really does.

   (*throws penknife.*)

See, that's pretty nice. It's very undramatic like that. Very banal, isn't it?

It doesn't look like someone put it there. It almost looks like it fell out of someone's pocket as they reached for something else.

Yeah, but see, when it's too casual, when we don't do any arranging at all, that also suggests that someone just dropped it.

Yeah.

What if we tuck it into the folds a bit more?

(*tucks the penknife into the folds.*)

Mm-hm. Yeah, that's really nice.

But see, now the problem is that it looks like it was left there specifically to be found.

Like a warning?

Yeah.

Yeah, you're right. It's too much like a sign. Something that wants to be found.

Okay, well, what if we made the whole scene messier, so there wasn't so much focus on the knife? I mean, could we, I don't know, put the pillow under the duvet or something?

What do you mean? Oh, like remake the bed so that it's—

So it's messier.

Ah, I get it. That's not bad, actually. That's a good idea.

I'll try.

(*remakes the bed so that it's messier. flaps the sheets.*)

But now it just looks like someone's just had a really crazy night, doesn't it?

What about another element that works against the mess? Something really deliberate. Like, what if I roll up the end of the duvet?

(*starts rolling up the end of the duvet.*)

But roll it only partially.

(*stops rolling it up, so that it's only partially rolled up.*)

Sure. Like that?

Yeah, like that.

And then what if the penknife is nestled just a bit under the twist?

(*nestles the penknife under the twist.*)

Oh, that's a little scary.

It's a little bit nastier, huh?

Yeah, now it's getting monstrous.

It's not as good.

You think it's too much?

Yeah.

I mean, yeah, there's something to it, but it's not as good.

It's too mannered, isn't it? Now the penknife is just part of this ridiculous theatre, rather than…

Right. The whole scene really draws attention to itself.

Yes.

And that might lead to people thinking that someone put it there, whereas when the knife was kind of resting in the little puffed-up cloudy divot, that felt so innocent that you didn't really think about someone being behind it…

Yeah, this looks like a whole arrangement.

Yeah…sorry…

No, no, it was a good idea.

Let's try something else. What have we not tried?

We could just stab it, right? Or cut the bed up.

No, nothing like that.

Of course not.

No.

I was just kidding.

Can we do something to the pillow?

Like what?

The pillow's very puffed-up. Could we knock the air out of it?

Yeah, how can we make it as flat and lifeless as possible?

Punching it?

That's not bad.

>　(*punches pillow.*)

Punch the other side too.

>　(*punches the other pillow.*)

Now it looks like two heads were sleeping on the one pillow.

Yeah. Or two cats.

Or two cats.

Eh. It's a bit...referential.

What if I also pinch the pillowcase (*pinches pillowcase*), like this, so there's a little pinched peak, and put the penknife next to it?

Hm.

That's nice, but it looks deliberate.

Yeah.

But I like the pinch, that's a good direction, let's try it somewhere less conspicuous.

What if we pinched all around the edges, at intervals?

No, that's too systemy.

Yeah, that would definitely seem intentional.

I like the idea of doing something on the edges, though.

Okay, I have an idea. What if...it's hanging over the edge of the bed as much as it can without falling off?

Huh. Not a bad idea. I'll give it a try.

> (*balances the penknife so that it hangs over the edge of the bed.*)

Yeah, like that, but it's not on the edge enough.

It's hard to get it to stay—

It needs to look like it's almost impossibly balanced.

Yeah—

(*still trying to balance it.*)

Most of it should be hanging over the edge. More than half of it, if possible. It should look like it should have fallen already.

(*more attempts at balancing.*)

Right. I get the idea. But it's not working.

Let me try.

Sure.

(*tries to balance it, the same thing happens, it falls.*)

Oh, I almost had it.

(*tries again.*)

Almost—

Almost.

(*tries again.*)

Oh, almost.

Yeah, but not quite. Yeah, I don't think it's going to happen.

No, I don't think so either. It would look really convincing, though, if it did.

It would look incredible.

There is a large flat-screen TV standing upright on the floor, near the living room area. It is angled more for the audience than the actors. The actors can see it, but the audience can see it better.

When turned on, it plays live TV. Whatever is on, is on the TV. It is on for most of the second half.

Acting

flat and low acting.
the actors keep their eyes among themselves, and not at
the room or the audience.
the actors' voices should be as quiet as their proximity
dictates.
things can be just a bit funny. funny as in off.
they make gestures that are normal for talking to friends.
little tics and touching and stuff. fiddling a little with
the beer bottles or themselves.
the beer bottles and grapes are there to be touched and
consumed for real.

in the second half, when PETER *is alone, his movements*
are very precise. there is a submerged hint of dance to them.

it is important to give the actor playing PETER *the*
direction: he is not sad.
he might be sad, who knows, but the actor should not
think of him as specifically sad.

Bed

The sheets of the bed continuously writhe, noiselessly, in no discernable pattern.

> *three long metal axles in the frame of the bed.*
> *each long metal axle skewers four deformed wooden circles.*
> *the long metal axles are attached to motors that make them spin really slowly.*
> *a controller with volume-like knobs on it controls the speed of the spinning.*
>
> *there is no mattress on the bed, but instead there are a number of sheets stapled into the frame of the bed, to make it look like it has the thickness and give of a mattress.*
> *on top of that, there is a clean set of white bedding, a duvet, and two pillows.*
> *as the deformed wooden circles turn, they nudge the sheets.*
> *the duvet and pillows rise and fall gently with the nudging.*

The bed is positioned on the edge of the stage, at an angle to the stage so that only one leg of the bed is on stage. This leg is cut to compensate for the differing heights of stage and not-stage.

Writing
bed mechanism.

Credits for first production

SCRIPT, CONCEPT,
DIRECTION, AND SET DESIGN
Ed Atkins and
Steven Zultanski

CAST
Lotte Andersen, Peter Christoffersen,
Ida Cæcilie Rasmussen

CHOREOGRAPHER
Nønne Mai Svalholm

THEME TUNE
Lawrence Giffin and
Steven Zultanski

ASSISTANT DIRECTOR
Pernille Hviid

STAGE MANAGER
Anne Kirstine Pyndt

CO-PRESENTER
CPH:DOX

SOUND ENGINEER
Anders Munch Amdisen

LIGHTING DESIGNER
Karl Sørensen

MASTER ELECTRICIAN
Peter Lorichs

MASTER CARPENTER
Rasmus Rahbek

HEAD OF COSTUMES
Kristina Widriksen

PRODUCTION MANAGER
Svend Martin Holst

BUILDER
Andrew Mathews

THEATRE PLUMBER
Kenneth Kreutzfeldt

PRODUCTION ASSISTANT
Emma Dybdahl Hildebrandt

CHIEF DRAMATURG AND
CURATOR
Rikke Hedeager

TRAILER
Sara Galbiati and
Jonas Skovbjerg Fogh

FUNDING
Wilhelm Hansen Fonden and
Beckett-Fonden

THANKS TO
Signe Lausen, Anders Astrup Jensen,
Rune Klan, Hollis Pinky Atkins,
Sally-Ginger Brockbank,
Ida Marie Hede, Henriette Heise,
Chris Shields, Finn Hagen Storgaard

Ed Atkins has exhibited internationally, including solo presentations at New Museum, New York; Serpentine Gallery, London; Martin-Gropius-Bau, Berlin; Castello di Rivoli, Turin; Stedelijk Museum, Amsterdam; TANK Shanghai; and MMK, Frankfurt. He is the author of *Old Food* (2019) and *A Primer for Cadavers* (2016), both published by Fitzcarraldo Editions.

Steven Zultanski is the author of several books of poetry, including *Relief* (Make Now Press, 2021), *On the Literary Means of Representing the Powerful as Powerless* (Information as Material, 2018), *Bribery* (Ugly Duckling Presse, 2014), and *Agony* (Book*hug, 2012). An essay, *Thirty-Odd Functions of Voice in the Poetry of Alice Notley*, was published as a pamphlet by Ugly Duckling Presse in 2020.

( )　(　　　　　)　　p　　prototype

poetry / prose / interdisciplinary projects / anthologies

Creating new possibilities in the publishing of fiction
and poetry through a flexible, interdisciplinary approach
and the production of unique and beautiful books.

Prototype is an independent publisher working across
genres and disciplines, committed to discovering and
sharing work that exists outside the mainstream.

Each publication is unique in its form and presentation,
and the aesthetic of each object is considered critical
to its production.

Prototype strives to increase audiences for experimental
writing, as the home for writers and artists whose work
requires a creative vision not offered by mainstream
literary publishers.

In its current, evolving form, Prototype consists of 4
strands of publications:
(type 1 — poetry)
(type 2 — prose)
(type 3 — interdisciplinary projects)
(type 4 — anthologies) including an annual anthology
of new work, *PROTOTYPE*.

Sorcerer by Ed Atkins & Steven Zultanski

Published by Prototype in 2023

'Two People Attempting to Place a Penknife on a Bed so
that It Appears as if No One Put It There' was originally
published in the *Chicago Review*. Thanks to the editors.

A CIP record for this book is available from the
British Library.

Designed by Joe Hales
Typeset in Haultin
Printed in the UK by TJ Books

ISBN 978-1-913513-49-8

(   )   (   )   p   prototype

(type 3 – interdisciplinary projects)
www.prototypepublishing.co.uk
@prototypepubs

prototype publishing
71 oriel road